What Is Justice?

a personal exploration

Bill Denham

What Is Justice?
a personal exploration

©2019 by Bill Denham

Fernwood Press
Newberg, Oregon
www.fernwoodpress.com

All rights reserved. No part may be reproduced
for any commercial purpose by any method without
permission in writing from the copyright holder.

Acknowledgments
> *Looking for Matthew*; *December's eyes*; *O Felix culpa*, *Oh, light from darkness*; *The emerald flash* all come from the small book of poems titled, *Looking for Matthew* (Apocryphile Press, Berkeley, CA, 2012).

Other Publications by Bill Denham
> Poetry
> *Looking for Matthew*, (Apocryphile Press, Berkeley, CA) 2012
> *of gossamers and grace*, (Finishing Line Press, Georgetown, KY) 2016
> *death will come*, (Fernwood Press, Newberg, OR) 2018

Interior and cover design by: Mareesa Fawver Moss

Printed in the United States of America

ISBN 978-1-59498-057-2

Contents

What Is Justice?
    Part I   7

The nature of being human
    Part II   21

We are not innocent
    Part III   29

Compassion—a radical critique
    Part IV   41

Imagination
    Part V   53

Epilogue   59

Acknowledgments   61

Notes   65

Biography   69

What Is Justice? a personal exploration—

is an engaging, deeply personal and deeply felt exploration into the meaning of the word, justice, triggered by the arrest of three young Hispanic men who have been charged with the capital crime of murder—for the deaths of Matthew Avery Solomon and Noel Espinoza on September 4, 2008, and so they face the death penalty. Incorporating a number of his own poems, Denham is unflinching in his self-critique and in his critique of our broader culture and the system of retributive justice it pursues suggesting an alternative system based upon our inter-connectedness and upon exercising our imagination—an essential, thought provoking piece.

Additional praise for *What Is Justice?*

"What does it mean to love our enemies? I know of no better answer in our time than the care Bill Denham shows the men who killed his stepson. With vulnerability and courage, he uses a poet's ear and a prophet's eye to redefine justice. His story moved me deeply."

Bruce Murphy
retired as President at Northwestern College, a former Pastor at La Jolla Presbyterian Church and Bethany Presbyterian Church

"Bill Denham has given us a gift in a few short pages. As he shares his experience of losing someone he loves to violent death, he invites us to accompany him as he searches his own heart and enters as he can into another's experience. The insights he gathers into his poetry, prose, and the quotations he incorporates challenge us to do the hard work of subverting the systems that numb us by learning compassion for the other."

Becky Ankeny, Ph.D.
Recorded minister in Sierra-Cascades Yearly Meeting of Friends

What Is Justice?

Part I

September 4, 2008, to September 4, 2018—a decade, ten years—September 4 being an anniversary of a murder, the murder of Matthew Avery Solomon as he walked the streets of San Francisco with his two young friends, Noel and December, after work, just hanging out and having a good time.

As it turns out, just a few months ago, in the middle of this tenth year, three young Hispanic men were arrested and charged with the murder of Matthew and of Noel, his buddy. December survived to tell the story:

December's eyes

Her ears ringing from the shots,
    she could not hear herself scream,
    "They shot Matt and Noel!"
    "They shot Matt and Noel!"

People turned from the bar,
    looked up from their conversations
    as if they could not understand
    what they saw and heard—
    this young woman
    standing in the doorway,
    calling for help,
    not knowing she, too, had been shot,
    blood flowing down her arm
    her sweatshirt clinging
    to her flesh.
    Or perhaps they did know,
    all too well, what they saw
    and did not or could not move.

She tracked their eyes, looked down at her arm,
    turned and ran back to her friends,
    who lay in pools of blood—
    Matt dead, Noel dying as police arrived.

They told her Matt was dead, tended to Noel,
and loaded the two of them and Matt's body
into the ambulance.

Noel died, too,
    but December, that was her name,
    lived to tell the story
    of the three of them hanging out after work—
    Noel doing his karaoke thing
    while she and Matt cracked up.
    She spoke of their decision
    to cruise the street when the next act up
    was a country western.
    They were just hanging out, being friends,
    walking back and forth a bit,
    and she sat down on a Muni bench—
    the three of them, joking and playing around,
    helping each other in that way,
    never suspecting a thing.
    Then the shots rang out—and it was done.

The two masked gunmen, she was told,
    got in a van and drove away.
    She never saw them.
    But her eyes, now, her beautiful eyes,
    have a look that's hard to hold—

not glazed over, not shut down.
They're simply eyes that know,
know exactly what they've seen.

Day 16, September 20, 2008 [1]

Saturday, April 7, of this year (2018) at 10:16 PM, I received a text message from Ken Solomon, Matthew's adoptive father. It says, in part:

> "Hey there, Bill. Got a call from Homeland Security they caught 3 men who were responsible for Matt's death. They said they were targeted ... gang related. Don't know anything else."

Over the next six weeks I talked with friends and with my son, Leslie, and with friends in the Redwood Men's community, and I searched online for the indictment which I found and read.

My son told me he had spoken to a Homeland Security person who had given him the name of a "victim's counselor." He had called the number and left a message and never received a return call. He told me that after thinking about it he had decided to not attend the trial, seeing no benefit for himself in doing so.

I brought my concerns about the accused young men to the annual men's conference at the Mendocino Woodlands camp number two over the Memorial Day Weekend. The theme of the conference was "walls." During our exploration of the various walls we construct for ourselves, by our own psychology, or walls that are constructed by our broader culture, we talked about the language of walls. One phrase that

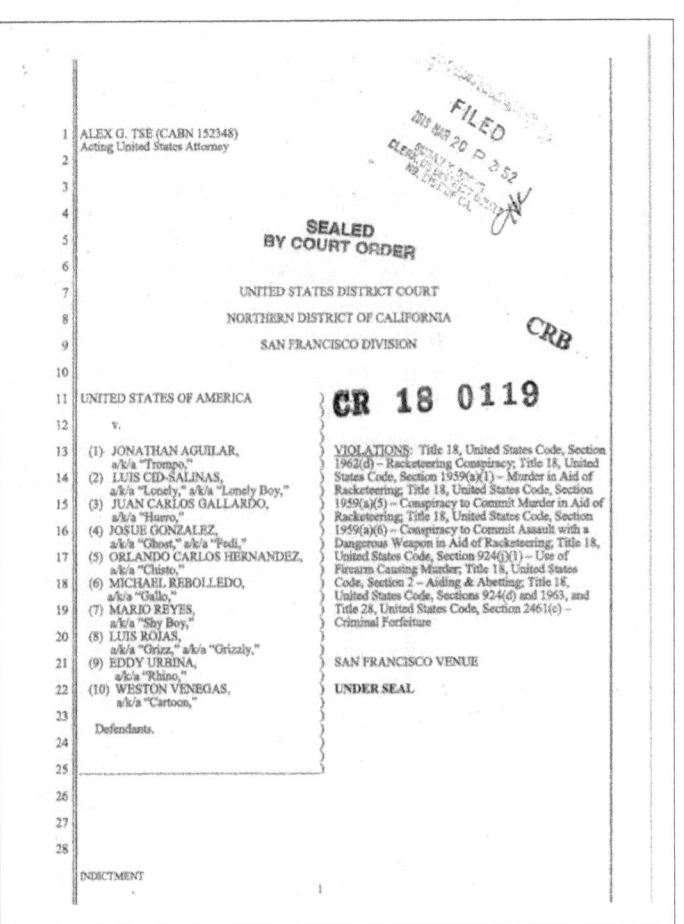

The indictment filed by Alex G. Tse, Acting United States Attorney in the United States District Court on March 20, 2018.

stuck with me was "up against the wall." In our last open circle, I confided that I felt up against the wall in three areas of my life, one of which was how to negotiate the Bleak House-nature of the federal judiciary system. How would I be able to find these young men and hopefully begin a conversation with them? The task seemed overwhelming.

I'm not sure when or how the idea came to me, but during that first week of June after I had gotten home to Portland, Oregon, the thought occurred to me to look for the defense attorneys for these three young men—Josue Gonzalez, Eddie Urbina, and Luis Rojas. They were being charged, I later learned from one of the defense attorneys, with a capital offense, since the Justice Department was prosecuting them under the federal racketeering act. San Francisco Police Chief William Scott said of the arrests, "We hope that these arrests will bring a measure of comfort and healing to the families of the victims, many of whom have waited years for justice."[2] But somehow, to me, seeking the death penalty did not feel like justice. How could state sanctioned murder be just? It could only be considered just in a retributive system—an eye for an eye, a life for a life. The way I look at this world, that has nothing to do with justice. From my point of view, the concept of justice involves doing right by someone or some thing, and doing right by someone or some thing means taking care of, doing right by each party—victim and perpetrator. It does not mean there are no consequences for the harm done. It simply means recognizing the humanity of each participant and exploring together how to resolve the issue.

Luis, Josue, and Eddy are accused of doing wrong, perhaps the gravest of wrongs, ending the life of Matthew and that of Noel, taking an entire lifetime away from them. And in

Matthew's case, taking a father away from two young sons. Does it not seem reasonable to ask of them to give up their own lives to make it right, to balance the scale, so to speak?

I don't think so.

That punishment looks like revenge.

No one is helped.

In the case of a murder, where a life has been taken, the survivors of the victim may get a momentary sense of satisfaction when the perpetrator is killed by the state and the state declares that "justice is done," but that satisfaction does not last because revenge is not a motive that comes from our "better angels," which is to say from our emotionally mature selves, but from our worst angels, those parts of ourselves that desire to hurt another, from our anger and from our hatred, two emotions that are understandable when a loved one has been killed. These are not emotions that we act upon if we are interested in achieving justice. Justice does not come from anger, nor does it come from hatred.

So, what is justice?

Let's think about a metaphor, a metaphor that was introduced by Valarie Kaur in a TED Talk entitled, *Three Lessons of Revolutionary Love*.[3] What if the darkness we are experiencing—whether it is the darkness of our present political climate or the darkness surrounding this murder or some other darkness—what if, she asks, it is not the darkness of the tomb—the darkness of death—but the darkness of the womb; what if it is the darkness that proceeds birth? If we look at life in this way, it forces us to ask another series of questions, starting with "What can be born from this darkness—this tragedy?" It demands that we look carefully at what are the needs of each individual involved in this experience. What are my needs, as one who cared for Matthew? What are Matthew's two sons' needs? What are Matthew's siblings' needs? What are the mothers of Matthew's two sons' needs? What are the accused perpetrators' needs? What can they do, if they are guilty, to help repair the damage they have done?

In early June, as I said, I searched for and found the names and addresses of the three defense attorneys for Josue, Eddie, and Luis. And I started my own private search for justice by writing each attorney a letter. Here is a copy of that first letter.

Subject: Indictment Filed Under Seal 180320 (002) by Mission Local on Scribd (missionlocal.org)

> 22. The defendant, LUIS ROJAS, a/k/a/ "Grizz," a/k/a "Grizzly," has been a member of the 19th Street gang since at least 2003. Among the ways in which he participated in the conduct of the affairs of the enterprise are the following. He has carried firesrms (sic) and commited (sic) assaults in gang territory. On September 4, 2008, in the vicinity of 24th and Utah Streets in San Francisco, ROJAS, along with gunman EDDY URBINA and getaway driver, JOSUE GONZALEZ, shot and killed Victim-4 and Victim-5, who they believed were rival gang members, in retaliation for the murder of a fellow gang member earlier that day. In this same shooting, Victim 12 was wounded ...

Dear Ms McClure,

I found your name online and I have visited your website, read the entire thing.

I am Bill Denham, a 76-year-old retired letterpress printer, living in Portland with my wife, June.

On September 4, 2008, I was living in Berkeley on MLK, north of University Avenue, in a small cottage behind World Without War Council. Matthew Solomon had lived there with me for about a year after he had gotten out of prison. His adoptive mother had rejected him and his adoptive father was then living in Canada. I was the only person Matthew had—so much so, that the police called me when he was murdered that day. They had found my name and number in his wallet. Though I have no legal familial relationship with Matthew, I call him my step-son because I was a part of an extended family that he grew up in and I functioned in a parental role with him. I knew him for 20 of his 23 years. He was adopted at the age of three—a conscious, painful memory for him.

I am a poet. After Matt's murder, I processed his death, the grief I felt and the responsibility I felt for his death through my poems and in 2012, I wanted to honor Matt's life by making something beautiful. So I designed and letter press printed 55 copies of seventeen lyric and narrative poems in the form of a hand stitched book that chronicle my responses, my thoughts and feelings about his death.[4] "the apocryphal press" in Berkeley offset printed 500 copies of the small book.

In the introduction to the book, I talk about my feelings upon receiving the police officer's call:

> Yet even as I felt the numbness come over me and knew the rage and sorrow that were to come—I am no stranger to loss—I knew a far greater grief, beyond the personal, a profound sadness for the lives of the two young men who murdered Matthew—two young men who must live without hope, like thousands of others, who see no future for themselves and have little regard for life—their own or another's.

So, I am writing to you to ask for your help. I would like to get in touch with your client and the other two young men who are accused of killing Matthew and Noel and wounding December. First of all, I wonder if these accusations are accurate. Secondly, if they are accurate I would like to send Luis a copy of my book and see if we can't have a conversation. I am not interested in retributive justice. I much prefer restorative justice. I would appreciate any help you can give me. If you would like I can send you a copy of my little book to the address below?

Thanks and blessings,

Bill Denham

PS: Here's a copy of the title poem for the book:

Looking for Matthew

He's gone ... he is gone ...
    yet, we must look for Matthew ...
    we must look for Matt
    where we can find him—
    in Jayvion and in Makai, of course,
    in that genetic and physical kind of way,
    but in ourselves, as well,
    in that other kind of way,
    in that way that's always true,
    in that way that you are another me
    and I am another you,
    and there, in that place,
    I see myself in Matt
    and Matt in me
    and not just in the smile,
    the determination,
    the vision of what might be,
    for Matt and I
    shared all that
    but shared, as well, much more—
    the struggles, the darker side
    that sometimes brought us low
    but never held us there.
    So I look for Matt each day,

where, now, he lives—
inside of me and I say,
"Whassssup bro?"
and he gives me
that look of his—
a gift, in my mind's eye,
that'll carry me,
carry me through
another day.
It's all I
can do
but still
I hurt,
still I
cry.

9/22/2008

Matthew Avery Solomon, my stepson, was shot and killed while walking with friends on a San Francisco Street on September 4, 2008, an innocent victim of some gang related retaliation. His friend Noel Espinoza was also killed.

Matthew Avery Solomon

March 3, 1985—September 4, 2008

Photograph taken a week before his murder.
Matthew was Employee of the Week at Goodwill.

An unexamined life is not worth living.

          Socrates—399 BC

Nothing is so difficult as not deceiving oneself.

         Ludwig Wittgenstein—1938

The nature of being human

Part II

All three defense attorneys responded positively to my inquiry, expressing sorrow for my loss. I thanked them for that expression but stated my current and long-time desire to explore ways to turn this tragic mistake into something positive.

I have sent each of them copies of *Looking for Matthew*.

I have been counseled that the pace of such litigation is glacial, at best, and that the capital charges—the death penalty—in the indictment may never be sought. Regardless, I am hopeful that at some distant point in time I will be able to share Matthew's story with Luis, Eddie, and Josue.

Maybe I will be able to figure out some way for us to be in contact with each other.

In my research, reading about various cases on the Death Penalty Information Center website (deathpenaltyinfo.org) and reading books like Bryan Stevenson's *Just Mercy*, I was surprised but pleased to discover that the Justice Department provides the funding for an adequate defense—meaning an examination of the accused's life and family for three generations back—how much funding and how that level of funding compares with the federal funding for prosecutors—I didn't discover.

But, let us return to our consideration of the nature of justice.

It looks like the retributive system of justice, especially in capital cases, is based upon making a distinction between the perpetrator and the victim, based upon erasing what they have in common, their sameness, their essential humanity, robbing both of that fundamental truth—we are all human beings. We are all made in the image of God—perpetrator and victim. When this truth is denied, we are unable to seek justice. We are limited. We limit ourselves. And from this limited place we can only define justice as retribution—an eye for an eye—as revenge, as punishment for the wrong doer. In capital cases, that punishment becomes state-sanctioned murder, the legal killing of another human being.

I am reminded here of a powerful poem by DH Lawrence:

> I am not a mechanism, an assembly of various sections.
> And it is not because the mechanism is working wrongly that I am ill.
> I am ill because of wounds to the soul, to the deep emotional self and wounds to the soul take a

>
> long, long time, only time can help and patience, and a certain difficult repentance,
> long, difficult repentance, realisation of life's mistake, and the freeing oneself from the endless repetition of the mistake
>
> which mankind at large has chosen to sanctify.

State-sanctioned murder—a life for a life—and war are the mistakes that "mankind at large has chosen to sanctify." Both seem to separate us from the perpetrator or from the enemy, elevating us while denigrating the other, making them into something other than human. We see ourselves as a person, a human being, and in whatever ways we decide to define the perpetrator or the enemy, we see them as something other than human, other than ourselves. We make them into "the other" and feel justified in taking their life.

We profess ignorance and even shock, asking, "How could anyone do this horrible act?" Or "how could this group of people not value the sanctity of human life?" They are so different from us. They are so different from me.

Oh, how we speak, at such times, out of both sides of our mouths.

A universally human response—we project those dark parts of ourselves that we are unable or unwilling to examine or even to acknowledge onto another person or onto a group of people, relieving ourselves of the necessity of examining our deepest and innermost fears and dark urges, thereby living what Socrates calls "the unexamined life." Such an unexamined life contributes to attitudes of self-justification, of self-righteousness, which, to use Wittgenstein's term, is a "self-deception," a failure to see that we are all alike—all equally capable of doing great good and of doing great harm—and as he says, "Nothing is so difficult as not deceiving oneself."

This is the nature of being human.

This must be the starting point of any consideration of justice because justice rises from truth and humility.

Justice incorporates an acceptance of each person's humanity, regardless of the harm that has been perpetrated—even if a life has been taken, even if our desire is to take the perpetrator's life in return. We must be able, if we are seeking justice, to examine our desire to trade a life for a life, to recognize our own ability to change, to forgive, and to recognize as well the perpetrator's ability to change, to ask for forgiveness.

If we return, then, to Valarie Kaur's metaphor of the darkness of the womb, and if we accept that each person involved in the killing of Matthew and Noel—all three of the accused perpetrators and all of the survivors—are all human beings—we must try to determine what would be a just outcome for each individual. If those accused of the murder are, in fact, guilty, what do they need to do to help themselves restore their own humanity, some part of which was lost even before they took the life of another? How can they restore that part of themselves? How can they make recompense? And for those of us who were close to the victims, what are our individual needs relative to the loss of Matthew and of Noel?

O, Felix culpa!
    Oh, light from darkness!

In a split second,
    as is always the case,
    even as internal growth
    creeps as slowly
    as deep time, itself,
    my life changed forever
    and stayed, as well,
    more deeply
    the same.

A masked young man,
    a gun in his hand,
    pointed at the back
    of Matthew's head—close in,
    chose in that split second
    to move his index finger
    hardly half an inch—
    once, twice, three times more,
    and in that small act
    became executioner.
    Matthew lay dead on the street.
    Noel, his buddy, lay fatally bleeding.

How is it, then,
>   I pulled the trigger?
>   That is the only question.
>   And the only answer I know
>   is the story of my life,
>   the story of Matthew's life,
>   the story of Noel's life,
>   the story of this nameless young assassin's life.
>   For, in fact, we are all in this together.
>   We are inexorably one with the other.
>   That's just the way it is—
>   always the way it is.

I know nothing
>   of the executioner,
>   nearly nothing of Noel,
>   save the profound agony
>   I saw in his immigrant parents' eyes.
>   I do know something of Matthew—
>   for twenty of his twenty-three years
>   I was in his life and formed it
>   in whatever ways I did—
>   for good or for ill.

But mostly I know myself,
> or more honestly, try to,
> and this nameless young man
> forced upon me in that split second,
> no doubt, thoughtlessly,
> the need for me to see
> myself as executioner—
> all those tiny
> infinitesimal
> acts that
> kill.
> *O, Felix culpa!* Oh, light from darkness!

Third Year, Day 78, November 21, 2010[5]

Your grandmother was not teaching me how to behave in class. She was teaching me how to ruthlessly interrogate the subject that elicited the most sympathy and rationalization—myself.

Here was the lesson: I was not an innocent.

Ta-Nehisi Coates,
Between the World and Me (2015)

We are not innocent

Part III

By the time Matthew was murdered in 2008, I had been ruthlessly interrogating myself for thirteen years. I am not entirely sure how I came to this excruciating effort by which I had gradually come to know myself—to know that I was not an innocent—to accept responsibility for the harm I had done to those I loved.

But three days after the murder, I awoke, and for a precious moment or two I forgot that Matt was dead. The realization that he was gone hit me, as I lay in a liminal state—half-awake/half-asleep—I saw that I had killed Matthew, that I had *"pulled the trigger . . . laid his body out cold and stiff/ on the coroner's table."*

The emerald flash

We stood on the deck together at the end of the day,
    high up the hillside in Pacifica, facing the Farallones,
    this young adolescent boy and me—quietly
    watching the sun slip into the sea,
    hoping to catch that rarest of moments,
    the emerald flash.
    And there it was!
    Astonishing! Brilliant!
    The fire red sun turned green—
    hardly a second—then gone!

Nearly ten years on, now, from that day
    and three more away from the muzzle flash,
    I wake in the pre-dawn dark
    and know a fleeting moment of grace—
    oh, blessèd moment of grace—
    before the terrible weight descends.
    Matt is dead! Gone in a flash!
    And I pulled the trigger,
    stole his warmth,
    laid his body out cold and stiff
    on the coroner's table—
    a liminal image
    frozen now—

    forever—
    in my
    mind.

Oh, how I know the truth of that—
    how I am alive, how Matt is dead.
    My boy is dead! He is my boy, yes!
    Though we shared not a single gene,
    his death is my weight to carry.

I hear your doubts, your wish to comfort

but hold your tongue and listen.
    Do not tell me I did the best I could,
    for I know the story, the whole story.
    Yes, we had spoken truth to one another.
    We had connected, healed to some degree,
    but blowback is forever,
    and in the end, our time too short,
    our efforts not enough.
    And here I am alive, my boy is dead.
    I am the adult, he was the child—
    this one's on me.

Yes, we saw that emerald flash together.
    Not knowing what made the fire go green
    nor how the end things would come,

> we loved the joy of beauty shared.
> And I hold that moment,
> as I hold Matt's body, cold,
> laid out on the coroner's table
> and know I have no time left
> to *try* to love myself.
> And I don't need to tell you
> how painful and how hard
> this work of love is!
>
> *Day 3, September 7, 2008*[6]

And so, two years and seventy-five days later—remember the poem at the end of Part II—*O Felix culpa! Oh, light from darkness*, November 21, 2010—I was able to see my liminal insight as a gift.

I was able to see that I was no different from Luis, Eddie, and Josue, though it would be another seven and a half years before I knew their names. I could see, if I interrogated myself, that even though I had never pulled the trigger and killed someone, literally, I had and I do kill metaphorically with each unfounded judgment I pass upon another, with the lack of caring attention for another, with each time my heart is closed to the suffering I encounter in my world, my ever-shrinking world.

It is true that I took Matthew into my home when he got out of prison, and it is true that we worked on healing our connection, on building trust. But even though I believe we made some progress in our efforts, that Matthew did believe I had changed from the person he had known as a young child—the enforcer in an emotionally abusive extended family, in which all the boys ended up in the criminal justice system and all the girls ended up with PhDs—an extended family made up of my first wife, her second husband, her ex-lesbian lover and mother of my second son, myself, and eight children—and even though Matthew did have my name and telephone number in his wallet when he was murdered, there were limits on his ability to trust me. When he was living with me, his second son, Makai, was born. I had no idea. We were not close enough for Matt to share that incredible experience with me.

In Matt's eyes, understandably, I was still someone who was not to be trusted.

So what has this to do with justice?

From my point of view, this is the starting place for justice—a world where each person is seen as a human being deserving of love and respect—both victim and perpetrator—where each person is seen as capable of doing great good and capable of doing great harm, where each person, through ruthless self-interrogation, takes responsibility for their own behavior—both good and bad. This point of view encompasses all of humanity. It crosses all cultural and political boundaries. It is the foundational basis for thinking about the question: what is justice?

Nearly eight and a half years ago in Tallahassee, Florida, a young man, Connor McBride, shot and killed his fiancée, Ann Margret Grosmarie, following an extended fight that went on for nearly forty hours (https://www.nytimes.com/2013/01/06/magazine/can-forgiveness-play-a-role-in-criminal-justice.html). Connor turned himself in to police. Ann survived the gunshot wound to her head but was only kept alive for four days on a ventilator. The first night in the hospital, Ann's father, Andy, was alone with his daughter. His wife, Kate, had gone home to try to get some rest. Andy, a devout Catholic, was praying and listening intently for his daughter to speak, to say something. Though her brain was dead, he "felt her say, 'Forgive him. Forgive him.'"

And though Andy felt his daughter was asking too much and there was no way he could forgive Connor, he kept hearing her request. Just prior to his and Kate's decision to turn off the ventilator, he became aware that it was Jesus Christ who was also asking him to forgive. It was this imperative and their close relation with Connor's parents, Julie and Michael, that led them to seek a restorative justice solution to the murder, something they had heard about from Allison DeFoor, an Episcopal priest, though the priest told them he had never heard of restorative justice being used in a murder case. Andy shared this conversation with Michael at one of their regular lunch get-togethers. And then Julie began an online search that turned up Sujatha Baliga, a former public defender who was the director of a national restorative justice project in Oakland, California.

This story is a story of possibilities, a story of human imagination.

It is a story of what can happen when people see each other as human, as essentially the same as themselves. When Andy saw that Michael had also lost his child. When Michael went to the hospital the night of the shooting and embraced Andy, though he had thrown up five times on the way. When Allison DeFoor spoke with Andy about restorative justice. When Julie, Connor's mother, created the opportunity for a restorative justice experience. When Sujatha Baliga agreed to help. When Jack Campbell, the Leon County assistant state attorney, was open to having a pre-trial restorative justice conversation among all parties—a conversation he later characterized as being "as traumatic as anything I've ever listened to in my life."

None of this could have happened without each person exercising their own imagination—putting themselves into the other person's experience. None of this could have happened without each person's ruthless self-interrogation.

Bishop Desmond Tutu told another story possibilities in his book, *No Future Without Forgiveness*—the story of the South African Truth and Reconciliation Commission (TRC). Bishop Tutu is an African Christian who speaks in an inclusive way about how all people are children of God. He also references the African concept of *ubuntu*—which might be loosely translated as "I am because we are." In other words, we exist only in relation to one another. We find our identity in that relationship to one another—how we respond to and treat each other. The TRC functioned, then, to give voice to the experiences of the victims of apartheid. It also allowed those perpetrators who were willing to take responsibility for their actions, to face their victims. This process allowed individual people, both perpetrators and victims to tell their stories—to be human in all the broadest ramifications of what that means—capable of doing great good and also capable of doing great harm.

Whether the story is of a restorative justice conversation in Tallahassee, Florida, in 2010, or of the testimony offered before the Truth and Reconciliation Commission in South Africa a decade and a half ago, the focus is on allowing ourselves to imagine that we are all connected by our humanity and that this binds us together and calls us to do the hard work of forgiveness and reconciliation.

I want you to think about something ... not something easy. I want you to imagine yourself in a difficult situation—this situation:

Imagine

Imagine this—
    an automobile tire
    hanging around your neck,
    resting on your shoulders,
    its weight forcing your head forward just a bit
    as if you were praying,
    which you may very well be doing—
    this tire filled with petrol
    and lit ablaze by your brother
    who does not feel ...
    who does not feel ...
    who does not feel like your brother
    who only feels that *you* are the *other*
    and so cannot feel ...
    himself.

Imagine this—
    the penetrating power
    of a face in flaming agony
    seeking the smallest crack or crevice
    in that self-constructed shell around a soul
    we know is there, somewhere
    behind the hand that held the match.
    Imagine that hand to be our own.
    Imagine that shell to be our own.
    Imagine that memory to be our own
    and follow that thought where it takes us.

Note: The practice is called necklacing. The first widely reported necklacing was in South Africa in 1985. The victim, Thamsanqa Kinikini, was believed to have been involved in corruption. Later that year, a twenty-five-year-old woman was accused of being an informer and was similarly killed.

I am a part of all that I have met ...

> Alfred, Lord Tennyson –
> *Ulysses*, line 18

Jesus in his solidarity with the marginal ones is *moved to compassion.* Compassion constitutes a radical form of criticism, for it announces that the hurt is to be taken seriously, that the hurt is not to be accepted as normal and natural but is an abnormal and unacceptable condition for humanness. In the arrangement of "lawfulness" in Jesus' time, as in the ancient empire of Pharaoh, the one unpermitted quality of relation was compassion.

Empires are never built or maintained on the basis of compassion. The norms of law (social control) are never accommodated to persons, but persons are accommodated to the norms. Otherwise the norms will collapse and with them the whole power arrangement.

Thus the compassion of Jesus is to be understood not simply as personal emotional reaction but as a public criticism in which he dares to act upon his concern against the entire numbness of his social context. Empires live by numbness. Empires, in their militarism, expect numbness about the human cost of war. Corporate economies expect blindness to the cost in terms of poverty and exploitation. Governments and societies of domination go to great lengths to keep the numbness intact.

Jesus penetrates the numbness by his compassion and with his compassion takes the first step by making visible the odd abnormality that had become business as usual. Thus compassion that might be seen simply as generous goodwill is in fact criticism of the system, forces and ideologies that produce the hurt.

Jesus enters into the hurt and finally comes to embody it.

> Walter Brueggemann,
> *The Prophetic Imagination*
> (2nd Ed. Fortress Press, Minneapolis, 2001)
> pp 88–89.

(Note: I have rendered the above single paragraph into five shorter paragraphs for emphasis.)

The history of America is not just pioneers and cowboys and inventions and business. It's also brutality and slavery and oppression. If we want the country to be better, we have to look at that history.

> Ijeoma Oluo,
> *White Lies*,
> The Sun Magazine,
> December 2018, p. 10

*Compassion—
a radical critique*

Part IV

In January 1943 my father volunteered to go to war as a chaplain in World War II. He served in the South Pacific in the Solomon Islands, and later in the Palau, the location of the deadly battle of Peleliu. My older brother Bob, who has researched my father's life, quotes a letter home from September 28, 1944, in which he says, "Watching the invasion from a mile or two offshore: 'war is *worse* than hell, and neither words nor pictures can describe it'."[7] Toward the end of his military service, on Memorial Day 1945, he wrote the following poem:

Voices from the Grave

Your day of triumph dawns o'er all the world.
Soon will the tyrants' banners be unfurled
No more. Their ignominious defeat
Shall mark your gloried victories complete.

Let now your knowledge of their damned design
To crush all freedom, and to undermine
The firm foundations of our noble State,
Keep strong your purpose, ere it is too late.

Remember long the brutal carnage done,
When you the present victory have won;
Forget not through the years those anguished cries,
That from the slaughtered innocent arise.

Keep ever fresh in mem'ry for all time,
Their ruthless, bloody carnival of crime.
Close not your minds to grim reality:
They're not all dead, nor their philosophy.

Not that in vengeance you must now repay;
(Revenge would only bring your own decay)
But that from evil memories of war,
Stern peace may enter through a guarded door.

The day of Brotherhood is not yet come.
(It may in some far-off millennium.)
Until it does, hold fast your present pain,
Or else we've died our battle-death in vain.

Several years later, as a young boy of ten or eleven years old, I have a distinct memory of listening to my father deliver a message from the pulpit of Southminster Presbyterian Church in Winston-Salem, North Carolina where he was the pastor. Looking around at the congregation, I was hit with the terrible awareness that no one was truly listening. I don't recall the specifics of the message, but in Brueggemann's terms, what I was witnessing was the "numbness" of the congregation. Admittedly, it was a ten-year-old perception, but it was the early '50s, just a few years after World War II and the seeds of the American empire had been well sown, something that President Eisenhower warned us against as he left office:

> "In the councils of government, we must guard against the acquisition of unwarranted influence, whether sought or unsought, by the military-industrial complex. The potential for the disastrous rise of misplaced power exists and will persist."[8]

Eisenhower's warning echoes my father's, though his focus is not upon external tyrants but upon the forces, internally, within our own nation, that had been set in motion by the mobilization for and the fighting of a "just war," where we could and would see ourselves as the good guys fighting evil.

Why, you might ask, are you talking about Jesus, World War II and Dwight Eisenhower in a piece about the nature of justice?

If we are to understand the true nature of justice, we must understand the current system of retributive justice and the culture that espouses it. We must apply Ta-Nehisi Coates' mother's commitment to teaching him ruthless interrogation of himself, not only to ourselves, individually, but to our entire culture. Only then will we see, as he saw, that we are not "innocents"—not individually nor as a culture. We must see how the history we tell ourselves about ourselves as a nation is full of "sympathy and rationalizations" that protect our concept of ourselves as innocent, as the good guys on the world stage.

We must tell ourselves the truth about who we actually are—in all of our goodness and in all of our terribleness. When we avoid telling ourselves the truth, we are prey to our shadows and are subject to our fears. We project onto others the terrible parts of our selves—our capacity to do untold harm—and find them to be less human, less than ourselves.

We are all subject to this false way of thinking.

It has no political boundaries. Telling the truth reveals our capacity for doing harm, when we think we are better than those we judge to be less than or evil or terrible. After all, the retributive justice system—an eye for an eye—is really no justice at all.

Such was the case—this way of false thinking—in the founding of our nation, where Europeans invaded the land, believing they were the instruments of God's will, which did not encourage any kind of "ruthless" self-interrogation, but rather promoted a self-justification for the taking of the land, for thinking of it as their own, and for the slaughter of its inhabitants.

> Those that scaped the fire were slaine with the sword; some hewed to peeces, others rune throw with their repaiers, so as they were quickly dispatched, and very few escaped. It was conceived they thus destroyed about 400, at this time. It was a fearful sight to see them thus frying in the fyer, and the streams of blood quenching the same, and horrible was the stinck and sente thereof; but the victory seemed a sweete sacrifice, and they

> gave the prays thereof to God, who had wrought so wonderfully for them, thus to inclose their enemies in their hands, and give them so speedy a victory over so proud and insulting an enemy.
>
> William Bradford,
History of Plymouth Plantation
(Boston, 1856)[9]

If we step back from this description, we can see the "sympathy and rationalizations" William Bradford employed to arrive at his conclusion that God had "wrought so wonderfully . . . to inclose their enemies in their hands." How convenient the belief that God is on their side. How justifying for the slaughter of "so proud and insulting an enemy." How relieving of any responsibility for their actions—for their taking of human lives—mothers, fathers, children, not to mention the land. Given this belief system, how difficult it would have been to see the Native Americans as human beings, deserving of love and respect, equally capable of doing good and of doing harm.

Carl Jung, following a trip to America, commented on this particular aspect of the American psyche. He "warned his students that when they analyze an American's 'shadow,' they must be . . . careful . . . 'because when the American opens a . . . door in his psychology, there is a dangerous open gap, dropping hundreds of feet, and in those cases where he can negotiate the drop,'"[10] that American will be faced with the "shadow" of genocide. Of course, the same would apply to those enslaved and stolen from Africa, through whose labor the wealth of this nation, this empire, was built. According to Ijeoma Oluo, this is a reality about who we are as a nation, that we have to acknowledge, if "we want the country to be better."

But as Brueggemann says, "Empires live by numbness . . . Governments and societies of domination go to great lengths to keep the numbness intact." As the quotation from William Bradford in the seventeenth century shows, this is how our nation started, and this is how it has proceeded until the present day where we have a president, the forty-fifth president, who embraces dishonesty, racial bigotry, and a lack of concern for the earth, as a way of life—no interest in, no pretense to telling the truth about himself or about the world we inhabit, which is really no surprise, given that he has inherited, as the elected head of state, a nation that Dwight Eisenhower cautioned against, a nation that has become an empire with a military presence in hundreds of bases around the world.[11]

So Brueggemann's view that the compassion of Jesus is a radical criticism of our current culture, including the implementation of retributive justice, offers us a way of thinking about a different kind of justice—a justice that is primarily relational and restorative—restorative of a connection, a relationship that has been broken, a justice that is based upon our interrelatedness, our connection with each other. But for us to access this connection in our current world of deep divisions, we must do the terribly difficult work of interrogating ourselves, searching out those places of dishonesty, of rationalization, of self-righteousness, all those things that we are afraid to acknowledge in ourselves but that identify us as human and connect us to our common heritage, our common cause, which is to care for each other and for the one small world we inhabit.

It fell to me

It fell to me.
    I don't know why.
    How can we know these things?
    It fell to me to dismantle,
    to take down the fortifications,
    to take apart myself
    not so to destroy
    but to try to understand,
    to hope to know
    the inner workings
    of a single human heart
    and go from there—
    to Auschwitz,
    for example,
    as an end point
    of all that brought us there,
    or as a new beginning for me,
    my own very private mirror
    that shows a heart quite able
    to morph such an image
    of unspeakable acts
    reflected there
    never, never to be done again
    unto others of their kind

that go unnoticed, unseen,
unrecognized as such
until their carnage has been done,
and then we say once more,
"Never again! Never again!"
to ourselves and go on—
to drones over Pakistan
for example, run by little boys
with joy sticks and video cams
from half a universe away
and think, no doubt,
if they think at all
of what they do,
of what we ask them to do
in our name and with our money,
think, no doubt, that they are fighting evil.
"A silly comparison," you say,
"Auschwitz and drones.
What have you learned
in all your dismantling
if this is where you end—
with drones and joy sticks?"
And where would you suggest I look, dear listener,
that I might understand more clearly
what I am complicit in—
East Oakland, perhaps?

Where, dear listener, would you look?
Where would you look?

And then we must listen.

A Way Forward

There is that of Christ
    in each of us,
    but none
    has the whole.

Therefore, we must listen,
    listen to discern
    what part we speak
    what part we hear
    what part is left unspoken.

We must not think
    our part is whole,
    nor another's part,
    nor the part left unspoken.

But searching our soul,
>   open to discovery
>   of something new
>   about ourselves,
>   hearing something new
>   from another,
>   being aware of something
>   yet to be spoken,
>   will lead us forward.

And what new thing
>   might we discover?
>   What fear uncover
>   that leads to deafness
>   and to judgment—
>   of ourselves or of another?
>   And how might owning
>   that part of us
>   and sharing
>   in faith
>   that we will be heard
>   and held as human,
>   show us the Spirit
>   and the way forward?

Under the new outlook multiplicity of material wants will not be the aim of life, the aim will be rather their restriction consistent with comfort. We shall cease to think of getting what we can, but we shall decline to receive what all cannot get.

M. K. Gandhi,
Young India,
3–9–25, 305

I do not believe in the doctrine of the greatest good of the greatest number. It means in its nakedness that in order to achieve the supposed good of fifty-one per cent, the interest of forty-nine percent may be, or rather, should be sacrificed. It is a heartless doctrine and has done harm to humanity. The only real, dignified, human doctrine is the greatest good of all, and this can only be achieved by uttermost self-sacrifice.

M. K. Gandhi,
The Diary of Mahadev Desai-I,
(1953), p. 149

[In Satyagraha] violence is eliminated and a Satyagrahi gives his opponent the same independence and feelings of liberty that he reserves to himself, and he will fight by inflicting injuries on his own person.

M. K. Gandhi,
Non-violent Resistance (Satyagraha),
Schocken Books, NY City,
1961, p. 20

Imagination

Part V

At the end of Part III, I asked something of you.

I asked you, using the imperative voice, to exercise your imagination.

You might say I gave you a command to imagine a horrendous scene, to imagine that you were a participant in that terrible act of necklacing, both as a victim and as a perpetrator.

I asked you to do this, understanding how difficult it may have been to do it, to help you see the underlying foundation of my understanding of the meaning of justice. If you found it too difficult to do, I would urge you to go back and try again. Try to put yourself in that situation, both as victim and as perpetrator.

For you see, imagination is the key component to the exercise of being just, of implementing justice.

Each person, in any given circumstance, must be able to imagine what the other person or persons' experience or experiences have been. In order to be able to do this, they have to be able to look at themselves honestly—no holds barred. This was the lesson I learned from Matthew's murder. Like Ta-Nehisi Coates, so taught by his mother's ruthless interrogation, I learned that I was not an innocent. From that liminal perception that I had pulled the trigger, that I had actually killed him, I was forced to look at myself and own how I had and how I continue, in actuality, to annihilate another when I pass judgment upon them without pursuing an understanding of who they are, without reaching out to them to listen. To hear their story, as Gandhi said, we must give the other "the same independence and feelings of liberty that" we reserve to ourselves. We must imagine that we are the same, regardless of the differing circumstances of our individual lives.

Without this kind of imagination, the compassion that Jesus felt for the marginalized and dispossessed could not happen. As Brueggemann said, "Compassion constitutes a radical form of criticism, for it announces that the hurt is to be taken seriously, that the hurt is not to be accepted as normal and natural but is an abnormal and unacceptable condition for humanness." So the hurt that arises from a system of retribution should not call forth from us further retribution—a life for a life—but should call forth from us an effort at understanding the origins of such hurt, not so to excuse or to discount the actual hurt but to help us, together—victim and perpetrator—come, jointly, to an imaginative solution.

In the case of looking for justice with Matthew's accused killers, I must be willing and able to exercise my imagination, to know that I am not an innocent, to first of all listen to their stories with compassion. I would also ask that they listen to mine, but the responsibility is initially upon me to establish the environment where these three young men—Luis, Josue, and Eddie—would feel comfortable enough, trusting enough, to speak honestly. This is a high order, for we are operating within a retributive justice system, a system that has no imagination, a system that asks us to punish wrong doing in a totally unimaginative way—an eye for an eye, a life for a life—no recognition of our humanness, of our ability to have an imagination, to have a life of the spirit, of our ability to learn, to grow, and to change. If we can get to this point—there are no guarantees that we will be able to do so—we can have a conversation.

We can explore ways that these three young men might be able to imagine a different way of living. I'm guessing that their lives have been lived in the shadow of our numb, dominant culture, embracing its retributive nature. According to the indictment, Matthew and Noel were killed "in retaliation for the murder of a fellow gang member earlier that day"—a life for a life.

For these three young men to arrive at a place of trust, when surrounded and subsumed by the dominant culture and their subculture, both of which operate without any affirmation of one's humanness, without any imagination, without any compassion, will be difficult. When facing the threat of retaliation, of execution, when facing their own deaths in exchange for the lives they have taken—to arrive at this place of trust will be a herculean task.

But it is the only task before me—the *only* task.

How could I do otherwise? How could I turn my back on our likeness, our humanness? How could I not give everything I am able to give to help these three young men to recognize themselves as human beings who have made a terrible mistake and to help them to have a genuine desire to change, to live their own lives in a more honest and conscious way.

Have I not been given the commandment to love my neighbor? Are not these three young men my neighbors?

If we can get to this point, we will have arrived at the beginning of a restorative justice process. What does that look like? I have no idea, but I am certain that it is the only path to justice in the murders of Matthew and Noel.

I am encouraged by the work of Valarie Kaur and her vision of revolutionary love, her embrace of the humanness of us all. In her recent conversation with Parker Palmer, they talk about the need for "open heart surgery" by which they are acknowledging the need for each of us to look inside ourselves, to discover what is there in all its complexities and messiness and then to bear our hearts, to become entirely vulnerable with each other, to trust that we will be seen and held as human.[12] Trust depends, I reiterate, upon our exercising our imagination and not giving in to our self-protective fear or our reflexive judgments, as a way forward within our broken, numb culture.

Imagine that!

On Christmas morning

To love is to love deeply.
    There is no other way.
    To love deeply is to suffer
    and to know suffering,
    for love comes only from an open heart—
    an open heart does not open here and close there.

There is, for sure, a powerful suffering that comes
    from closing one's heart, but being closed is being closed,
    closed even to the knowing of that pain
    that comes from our self-inflicted wound,
    our slamming of the door, whether from anger or from
        fear,
    from confusion or from ignorance, it makes no matter—
    a closed heart is closed, from the inside out and from the
        outside in
    and has no memory of what it is to be a heart—
    yet heart it has been, and heart it may be again—
    so always there is that hope.

Day 119, December 25, 2008

Epilogue

During the course of examining the nature of justice in these pages and in conversations I have had with others, people posed questions to me about my relationship with Matthew. I was forced to think about our entire history, about the actual limits of our connection when he was alive and how his murder and my sense that I was actually, quite literally, responsible for his death, allowed me to become aware of how centrally important Matt had become to my entire life. You might say that Matt's murder, the finality of his death and my sense of responsibility surrounding it, pushed him to the very center of my life, where he now sits, determining, in some sense, all of my actions—my intention to honor his short life by living absolutely the best life I am capable of living, and that, of course, now centers on these three young men—Luis, Josue, and Eddie—who have been charged with his murder. In his death, in the finality of that condition, his absolute absence, he has become much more central to my life than he was when he was alive.

The question, then, that I raise in this short essay is, "How can we turn this tragedy, this grievous error, this taking of Matt's life, this robbing his sons of their father—forever—how can we turn this tragedy to good?"

Acknowledgments

As is the case with anything I write, poetry or prose, none of which is, in any sense, original but is a gathering and a harvesting of thoughts and ideas that are in the world around me, that seem to me to be important, that need to be expressed within the context of my own personal experience and then shared as widely as I can manage, I hope, always, to be effective in encouraging others to live in this manner—examining their own experience critically, articulating the discoveries and sharing their observations with others as widely as is possible—for only in this way are we able to see each other as human. Of course, the other part of this kind of life is listening—listening with an open and non-judgmental heart.

The debts I owe are well beyond what I can list here, but let me express my gratitude for what I have learned from the three mothers of my children and what I have learned and continue to learn from my very own children. None of my present life would be possible without the love and support of my oldest and dearest friend, Sean Morris, thirty years my junior, yet one who has taught me how to live. Sean read the current manuscript and offered his critique that improved it considerably. Chris Morrissey and Dea Cox and Bruce Murphy also read and critiqued the manuscript.

To Kim Vanderheiden,[13] Bettina Pauly, and Mitsuko Baum, my colleagues at Painted Tongue Press in Oakland, California where I worked for years before my retirement and my move to Portland, Oregon, I owe a tremendous debt of gratitude for all the mentoring, teaching me how to be a letterpress printer, and for all the support around the original letterpress printed *Looking for Matthew*, whose edition of clothbound and boxed copies was Bettina Pauly's idea—an idea that she and Mitsuko Baum, both of whom are accomplished book artists, realized. They made fifteen copies of the fifty-five that were printed.

For my life, I am grateful to my mother and father who brought me into this world and gave me the best that they had to offer, and I am in very significant ways a combination of the two of them. To my older brothers, John and Bob, who have stood by me faithfully throughout my struggling journey, always supportive, never harsh nor critical, but patient and kind, I express my deepest gratitude for your presence in my life.

To the incredible group of conscious men of the Redwood Men's Center in Santa Rosa, California, whom I first encountered in the year 2000 at their annual conference, under the redwoods at Camp Gualala, where Robert Johnson, the Jungian psychologist, gave me a way to understand my life in terms other than the "good and evil" of my childhood and where Doug Von Koss spoke Mary Oliver's poem, *The Journey*, on Memorial Day in the *Temple of Melodious Sound* that set me on my own journey of becoming a poet once more.

To my wife, June, whose love of me as a young man, in high school, proved the greatest gift of a lifetime full of gifts—a gift of pure grace—whose poetic spirit and generous heart is always uplifting and sustaining.

Finally, to you, my readers, I owe everything to you, for without you I would be a lone voice crying in the wilderness. With you, we can move together toward realizing our own human potential, expecting the best of each other, expecting the best of our abilities.

Blessings,

Bill

Notes

1. Bill Denham, *Looking for Matthew*, (Berkeley, California: Apocryphille Press, 2012), *Day 16*.

2. Evan Sernoffsky, "SF police, federal agents announce indictments against alleged gang members," *SF Gate*, April 6, 2018, https://www.sfgate.com/crime/article/SF-police-federal-agents-announce-indictments-12813396.php.

3. Valarie Kaur, "3 lessons of revolutionary love in a time of rage," TedWomen 2017 video, 22:13 https://www.ted.com/talks/valarie_kaur_3_lessons_of_revolutionary_love_in_a_time_of_rage.

4   In order to design and hand print this tribute to Matthew, I had to raise the money to pay for it. Go to the following website to see the video, forty-six updates, seventy-eight comments, and childhood photos of Matthew: https://www.indiegogo.com/projects/looking-for-matthew#/.

5   Bill Denham, *Looking for Matthew*, (Berkeley, California: Apocryphille Press, 2012), *Third Year, Day 78*.

6   Bill Denham, *Looking for Matthew*, (Berkeley, California: Apocryphille Press, 2012), *Day 3*.

7   Robert Denham, *Memoir—My Father*, (unpublished manuscript), 24.

8   "Ike's Warning Of Military Expansion, 50 Years Later," NPR, January 17, 2011, https://www.npr.org/2011/01/17/132942244/ikes-warning-of-military-expansion-50-years-later.

9   Barry Spector, *Madness at the Gates of the City* (Berkeley, California: Regent Press, 2010), 156. The subtitle of Barry's book is *The Myth of American Innocence*. He analyzes in great detail the mythological underpinning of the stories we tell ourselves about our innocence. It's a book Howard Zinn calls "strikingly imaginative. This is truly an original work." Using Greek mythology and Carl Jung's psychology, Spector critically and brilliantly examines the stories we Americans tell ourselves in our culture's love affair with the notion that we are the exception, that we are innocent—how we project onto the "other" all our own worst fears and instincts about ourselves.

10 Elayne Wareing Fitzpatrick, *Traveling Backward: Curious Journeys and Quixotic Quests Beyond the Youth of Old Age* (Bloomington, Indiana: Xlibris, 2009), 354.

11 David Vine, "Where in the World Is the U.S. Military?" *Politico Magazine*, July/August 2015, https://www.politico.com/magazine/story/2015/06/us-military-bases-around-the-world-119321.

12 Valarie Kaur, "Session 7: The labor of revolutionary love," *Wisdom with Parker Palmer—Your Holiday Treasure Chest* video, 46:36, Posted December 6, 2018, http://valariekaur.com/2018/12/wisdom-parker-palmer-holiday-treasure-chest.

13 Justice Conversation (www.justiceconversation.org) invites viewers to study, share, and practice Justice as a concept rooted in Love. Kim is publishing *What Is Justice?* on her site in a series of serial posts. She is accompanying the posts by pieces of her own artwork, multimedia representations of Matthew, based on the photograph in this book.

Bill Denham
b. 1941

Educated in the South at Davidson College and at UC Berkeley in the mid-sixties where he received his MA in English Literature, he rejected a promising academic career after five years of teaching at Luther College and the University of Hawaii to go back to the land in the mountains of West Virginia. His subsequent journey of self discovery has been turbulent, painful but ultimately rewarding.

Now, in his late-70s, he is a retired letterpress printer from Painted Tongue Press in Oakland, California, where his collection of intricate paper sculptures still hang from the ceiling. He relocated to Portland, Oregon, in 2013, to be with an old high school classmate, June Quackenbush, after they reconnected at their 50th high school reunion in '09 in Winston-Salem, North Carolina.

He began writing poetry at the age of sixty after a forty-year hiatus from his youthful passion and he has written nearly 800 poems. He has published three small volumes of poetry—one in 2013, *Looking for Matthew*—seventeen lyric and narrative poems that explore his own grief and his own sense of responsibility following the street slaying of Matthew Avery Solomon on September 4, 2008, the second, *Of gossamers and grace,* in 2016—thirteen poems chronicling his late life love affair with his former high school classmate, and in 2018, *death will come*, published by Fernwood Press, an imprint of Barclay Press in Newberg, Oregon. His poem, *Do you remember, Dad?*, appeared in the anthology, *Daring to Repair* (Wising Up Press, 2012). Other poems have been shared widely among friends and colleagues at poetry salons and spoken word events and have appeared online over the years, primarily in his postings, *More morning musings from the land of the open heart*, through the list serve for The Redwood Men's Center (redwoodmen.org).

www.ingramcontent.com/pod-product-compliance
Lightning Source LLC
LaVergne TN
LVHW041309080426
835510LV00009B/918